Lost Among the Hours

Alan Britt

Alan Britt (signature)

11/1/18

▲

RAIN MOUNTAIN PRESS
New York City

Rain Mountain Press

New York City
USA
www.rainmountainpress.com
info@rainmountainpress.com

Joanne Bracken, Editorial Assistant

Layout & Design: Abecedarian Books, Inc.: www.abeced.com

Cover design and painting by Raúl Villarreal:
"No Longer (IN)Visible," acrylic & oil on canvas, 48" x 36"
Collection of the artist: www.raulvillarreal.com

ISBN-13: 978-1-4951-0606-4

Library of Congress Control Number: 2014955861

Printed by McNaughton & Gunn, Inc.
Saline, MI

Manufactured in the United States of America.

10 9 8 7 6 5 4 3 2 1

Lost Among the Hours

ACKNOWLEDGMENTS

The poems (sometimes in earlier versions) in this book previously appeared in the following publications. Grateful acknowledgment is made to the editors of those publications:

Ascent Aspirations Magazine (Canada): "Ode to Jackie Robinson"

Ann Arbor Review: "Jaguar" and "Giant Manuscripts"

The Bitter Oleander: "Bringing the World Together"

The Bond Street Review: "Various Disguises"

Calliope Nerve: "Wild Parakeets of Florida"

Camel Saloon: "Here Today," "Bob Dylan" and "Falling from Grace"

The Cultural Journal: "Beethoven's Eardrums"

Deep Tissue Magazine: "Friday Night, Late September," "Everyone Wants to Burn," "Getting Hard to Tell" and "After the Civil War"

Deuce Coupe: "The Ego" and "What Would Rumi Do?"

ditch: "The Corner of Edmondson and Northern Parkway" and "Various Disguises"

Exercise Bowler: "Evolution"

Flutter: "Magic"

Fullosia Press: "A Poem for Johnny Duckett"

Gloom Cupboard (United Kingdom): "American Politics"

Hanging Moss Journal: "Jimi Hendrix" and "The Appaloosa"

Hidden Oak: "Written Words"

Jones Av (Canada): "One More Time"

Ken*again: "Geronimo's Raid," "Partisan Objections," "Ultimate Innocence," "The Molar" and "For George"

The Minetta Review: "Yves Bonnefoy"

New Wave Vomit: "Pinot Noir," "Ode to Our Legal System" and "Good Fortune"

Omega: "Twist of Fate"

Osiris: "In-Between Lives"

Poetry Pacific (Canada): "Ode to a Movie Director" and "Shit Happens When You're a Dog"

Red Fez: "Ferris Wheel"

Sawbuck: "Shred of Evidence"

Scythe: "Friday Night, Late September" and "Getting Hard to Tell"

The Sound of Poetry Review (Greece): "Destiny," "A Quick Look at Despair," "For the Old Poets," "Marlon Brando" and "Rumi Speaks"

Tree Killer Ink (Canada): "In Love with the Universe"

The Tulane Review: "Pinot Noir"

Unlikely 2.0: "Lepers and Angels," "For Bob Dylan" and "A Sense of Humor"

The Unrorean (Broadside): "A Very Bad Poem"

Write from Wrong Literary Magazine: "Reading Poems," "The Lullaby Disguised as a String Quartet in C Major, Opus 59, No. 3, Razumovsky," "The Magic Poem" and "Rhetoric"

Write This: "The Frivolity of Language," "Lost Among the Hours," "Ariel" and "DNA"

Yellow Mama: "Poet to His Dog"

* * * * * *

"Wild Parakeets of Florida" and "In Love with the Universe" in *Parabola Dreams* (Poems by Silvia Scheibli and Alan Britt), The Bitter Oleander Press, Fayetteville, NY: 2013.

CONTENTS

"The River" by Paul Eluard (translated by Patricia Terry
and Mary Ann Caws)

(Part I)

(Part II)

Special thanks to Rob Cook and Stephanie Dickinson for their unflagging encouragement and support.

The River

The river that flows under my tongue,
The water no one imagines, my little boat,
And, with the curtains drawn, let's talk.

~Paul Eluard
(trans. by Patricia Terry & Mary Ann Caws)

Part I

I have only two certainties: that I was born alone without wanting it and that I will die alone without wanting it.

~Antonio Cisneros
(trans. by Ron Rodriguez)

Charles P. Hayes: "Moon Zongfixtures"

THE EGO

(*The ego simply disappears the moment you touch him.*)
                                    ~Kabir

Imagine diving
into daily existence
without intent
of finding something solid,
something rusted, perhaps,
but otherwise resembling an anchor,
say, from the *Wydah* or the *Santa Maria?*

My money's on the anchor, defending one
of the few sanctuaries we've got left.

And I'm not talking religion,
opiate to the masses,
although the ego must be stroked,
even during Midnight Mass.

The ego must be misunderstood like any good myth.

So, how do you caress the ego
without destroying it?

If Kabir had it figured out
600 years ago,
how come we're still
dealing with this problem?

JAGUAR

Black smoke rings—
flatbed Ford tattooing rainwater
onto stained, khaki nightmares.

(Like Congress could spell *khaki*
if their lives were bound and gagged
between the quivering hips
of 50-caliber gun sights.)

Jaguar squeezes copper eyes,
relaxes spotted shoulder,
licks her split saffron nose,
yawns,
then curls her golden head
into a long catnap.

GIANT MANUSCRIPTS

Some poetry manuscripts
are monster hurricanes
gripping the entire state
of Florida,
eerie eyes focused on West Palm,
Stuart and Ft. Pierce.

It just so happens
I dated a girl
from the Port St. Lucie corridor —
goldfinches igniting
quartz blue eyes —
but I digress.

These manuscripts, like elephants
spraying one another,
grow heavier and heavier,
down in our basements,
night after night.

Someday, with proper cultivation,
they could resemble
sperm whales 2 miles deep
trolling
their favorite meal,
the giant squid,
that elusive, mythical creature
whose 50-foot tentacles
occasionally litter
our shores of dementia.

WHAT WOULD RUMI DO?

Friend, I wish you wouldn't do that.

Friend, and I speak from experience,
you need to warn me
before arriving at my doorstep.

Perhaps it's better this way,
no festering neglects,
those dreaded sick roses.

Perhaps I'll ride that appaloosa
I've been dreaming
about these past six months.

Perhaps I'll even squeeze all
eight silk legs, friend, through
the neck of your favorite perfume
bottle, then squirt my defensive ink
from a purple felt-tip pen.

Yes, and someday Jesus,
mistaken for a homeless man
gripping a blue snow cone,
will share his holy melancholy
with the thirsty masses.

READING POEMS

(For Langston Hughes)

Your poem shattered sensibility.

Although poems are meant to rattle
our fairytale windows, they should
also boil our skeletons into a fine dust
sifting for signs of intelligent life.

But your poem, friend, with its sultry Harlem rhythms,
shivered the cactus spines of my soul.

Your poem kissed me
square on the mouth,
then invited me up to its room above a juke joint
where through sandalwood exaltations
we sipped black wine and enjoyed feral jazz.

We talked and talked about everything beneath the sun,
plus the torn and bloody quarter-moon,
until I joyously fell asleep.

*   *   *

Meanwhile, tonight, trapped inside habitual solitude,
I navigate a country road, dear friend, into a village of
nervous laughter and religious disgrace, into a metropolis
littered with three-piece 9-millimeters, fueled by my own
humble poems designed to rescue us all, once again,
from the latest, bigoted new world order.

LEPERS AND ANGELS

I'm not going to abandon
what I am.

This group of heretics,
this group
of lepers and angels.

This group of 21st century saints.

These saddened
and ironic poets
fueled by truth
who continue to write
their guts out.

I would no more
embrace the sentimental past
than I would join
those poor souls
who embrace the rose-colored future,
since evolution has given
us the gift of self-destruction
or salvation, and we are
one thin dime
away from the former.

THE LULLABY DISGUISED AS A STRING QUARTET IN C MAJOR, OPUS 59, NO. 3, "RAZUMOVSKY"

I love the idea of splashing
a late 18th century Bonn fountain,
especially with Beethoven scheduled to perform
right around the corner!

The anticipation is like waiting
for the next great Brando film
that never arrived.

But those violins . . .
each string a lexicon
of joyous melancholy!

Each string,
thin slices of Boar's Head roast beef, medium-rare,
Santoni's style,
with bass cello wagging its reptilian tail
across the halogen-blue asphalt of Alligator Alley.

Suddenly, the squawk of violins . . . like green parrots,
just as Velárde heard them.

Now I can finally put that Mexican lullaby to sleep.

That lullaby
buzzing my brain
these past 36 years!

FOR BOB DYLAN

(I gave up sewn clothes and wore a robe.)
                    ~Kabir

If we show respect,
they'll respond in kind,
just like any intelligent life form.

But if we highlight
their sins on the evening news,
the nasty side of things,
we'll sell more advertising.

The choice, of course,
is ours.

But, what if we in our walnut-paneled basements fall
in love with a Dutch servant girl sporting
one pearl earring, wandering nude,
after the family has gone to sleep?

One has only so much real estate . . .

So, *One day they blew him down in a clam bar in New York.*
He could see it coming through the door as he lifted up his fork.
He pushed the table over to protect his family.
And he staggered out into the streets of Little Italy.

Sister Jacqueline and Carmella
couldn't save us if they tried,
even though Jacqueline once crushed coquinas over
Richard's army blanket for eight straight mescaline hours.

But, seriously, what about the mythological god,
the one we saluted in grammar school?

Is he really short on cash?

Jesus.

Now, here comes this guitar, Bloomfield twanging
like a heart valve opening, closing, opening,
saying worship it your way, but worship it
like everyone's god-forsaken lives depend upon it,
which they do.

MAGIC

Our words shed misery
like shotgun cartridges
red as December holly berries
littering the boot prints
of childhood misadventures.

And happy words exist
for those who can afford them.

So, words, now, are hostages,
if I hear you correctly,
for this impossible life
to which we all aspire?

Ridiculous.

I say
strip the words down again,
like Lorca,
the greatest of all the warrior troubadours,
who died for us
puny civilians.

A SENSE OF HUMOR

A sense of humor doesn't hurt
all that much;
it resembles a Novocain needle
or a Lewis and Clark expedition
through the remaining vein reminding us
that life sucks.

Options, of course, are endless.

We could begin by removing land mines
from Bosnian pastures and Sudan villages.

Or we could publish unbiased history books
and reduce class sizes
in Baltimore schools.

Maybe we could send a few National Guardsmen
to Darfur, you know,
to reduce the raping and throat slashing.

National Guardsmen, the ones who survived Iraq.

So, what do you suppose we'll do when Iraq subsides?

Well, I'm not a weatherman,
but I'd say don your rubber lobster suit:
orange vest, orange suspenders,
orange hat.

Perhaps then you'll resemble
a caution light or a caesura.

At least you'll know
you're alive.

FERRIS WHEEL

What am I doing today,
outliving you?

That's not a fair cop,
now, is it?

Kinda like Barry Bonds
steroiding Hank's homerun record.

The carnival barker needs another shot
of meth.

The gypsy Ferris wheel
hesitates,
rocks
between rhyme and reason,
between thyme and razorblades,
before descending
back to religious ground.

WILD PARAKEETS OF FLORIDA

(For Duane Locke)

He parted the wall
so that we could enter.

He melted mortar from the bricks
supporting our future superstitions.

Ultimately, this allowed us to enter.

But, once inside,
we realized that genocide is a disease
more rampant than AIDS,
genocide ancient as DNA.

And now we're petitioning
what new stadium, exactly,
which new sports franchise,
while our children
slumped in overcrowded classrooms
are herded by underpaid sheepdogs?

This can't be why Blake
parted the Red Sea.

I'm telling you,
Blake was an escaped convict
from the 18th century
with nowhere else to go.

He reminds me of a poet
who once watched pale blue parakeets
blistering the pine trees
of St. Petersburg, Florida, 1969.

THE MAGIC POEM

(After Paul McCartney)

I'm 1/16th Cherokee
which makes me
one of those primordial patches
on a folk quilt.

And the burning quilt, burning
like nature intended;
well, I never told you
how much I loved you.

For that, I'll always regret.

Magic?

Perhaps if we suspend
our disbelief long enough,
anything's possible.

WRITTEN WORDS

Written words are deadly.

Like hollow-points shredding the chambers of unsuspecting
    brains.

You can't easily erase these deadly words
once they're lodged inside your brain
(unlike popular songs gulped in jubilation);
I mean, these words fuel genocide each Thursday in Liberia!

These words herded families into Viet Nam trenches.

These words, enslaved to financiers
by Special Forces
who in turn are slaves
to greedy
strands of DNA overflowing
our metropolitan graveyards.

But one thimbleful of written words can be deadly!

These words'll outlive nuclear tanks
and family fortunes built on refined oil
flowing beneath the sultry fenders
of GM's latest Cadillac
or Ford's nostalgic Thunderbird,
past electricity that once lit the Twin Towers,
past private stables with 25-year-old mares and geldings
dreading retirement sans any form
of equestrian social security.

So, today, I volunteer as legal counsel for all these verbs and
    adjectives
clomping their muddy paddocks of daily existence, snorting their
modicum of mischief, knowing full well that all I have to offer
are a few words like lexicon hollow-points rattling our skulls.

27

ONE MORE TIME

I gave myself to the universe.

What more can I give?

I'm down to one eye
and one lung.

If ashes from souls dumped into urns
are designed to nourish us,
why then do we still carry
nuclear clubs into heaven
and complain
about guardian angels
behaving like rented Geishas
in upscale Manhattan hotels?

Time to prison-break,
don't you think—
that is,
if time were
a lusty hourglass
with Pablo's
Isla Negra sand
feathering its crystal waist?

Part II

The judge's wig, however, is more than a mere relic of antiquated professional dress. Functionally, it has close connections with the dancing masks of savages. It transforms the wearer into another "being." And is by no means the only ancient feature which the strong sense of tradition so peculiar to the British has preserved in law. The sporting element and the humour so much in evidence in British legal practice is one of the basic features of law for archaic society.

~ Johan Huizinga

Charles P. Hayes: "Peekskill Umbrella"

RHETORIC

You know, some poems layered with banal abstractions
infiltrate every generation's canon,
while many poems about wonderful things,
goldfinches, leopard slugs, cuttlefish and wild vaginas,
get routinely overlooked.

Perhaps the time has come, friends, to sniff
with our noses,
not our brains!

A POEM FOR JOHNNY DUCKETT

Johnny, we got sidetracked
all these years.

But we had that Warren Spahn rosin bag
in our grips.

We saw Hank bullet three homers
over the institutional green wall at Connie Mack.

But that institutional wall,
like fate, with all her secret doors and jalousies,
who beckoned us to school dances at skating rinks,
was much taller than we expected.

We were only 12, then, Johnny.
Well, you were 14, but who's counting now,
now that our shadows loiter the slippery well
of death?

Today, we're fifty-something.

And Warren and Hank
are still the greatest we ever saw.

THE FRIVOLITY OF LANGUAGE

The frivolity of language, sometimes
in the hands of a culture's most esteemed poets,
apologizes for its obscurity.

Until rains, like the seasons, wash away
raspberry and lime hopscotch poems
from weather-beaten sidewalks.

Damn, once again, hunkered in my basement,
staring at a child's plastic bucket filled
with squatty, pastel chunks of chalk!

YVES BONNEFOY

Yves Bonnefoy assumes we already know this stuff
that plagues and perplexes. He, occasionally, like his

friend, Francis Bacon, strolls the moonlit curl of a dusty
question mark or trails blue sheep across the frozen

tundra of imagination. Yves shows us blood illuminated
by lightning and verbs that resemble swallows swarming

an abandoned church. He unhinges our bones, allowing
our souls to dip their exhausted hips below the black

waters of Lascaux. Yves Bonnefoy assumes we already
know this stuff that plagues and perplexes.

BRINGING THE WORLD TOGETHER

Deep down in the depths of our DNA . . .

If I were a caveman and saw you then,
I believe my chemical reaction
would've been pretty much the same
as it is today.

It might've been the smudges on your cheeks,
like those on Blake's chimney sweepers' cheeks,
or perhaps a fierce, green, Cuban wind
rattling tamarinds inside your bones.

In the depths of our DNA . . .

If I were a damselfly, wings pointing to the sky,
as I paused upon a smooth ax handle, watching
a July breeze rub her thighs against cucumber
pollen, or, perhaps, a leopard slug's beautiful
slime under moonlight.

LOST AMONG THE HOURS

(For Daphne)

She's probably chewing someone's underwear
right now,
that blonde Bouvier we prize so dearly.

These past six months the carved innocence
of her face has grown familiar.

Tonight she roams a section of our basement
unprowled by an adult dog
nearly two years, now, or is it four, already?

She's unaware she represents an entire generation
of fawn Bouvier des Flandres.

You can't blame her for that.

And when she really wants our attention,
she parades contraband across the living room—
white sock, dish towel carefully removed
from the back of a Scandinavian kitchen chair
or someone's sorrowful underwear
lost among the hours.

HERE TODAY

(String Quartet No. 14 in C sharp minor)

As I sit here today
I cannot say
if the east side
gets better sun
than the maple-infested west side
of my brain.

As I sit here today
I cannot say
whether or not
your confidant
is Iago
or someone
resembling him.

All I hear is a melancholy violin
igniting Beethoven's deaf quartet.

Ludwig hammered those strings
until they bled all over his music sheets.

And as Ludwig sits here today,
he cannot say
if Easter egg hunts are yet permitted
in the Count's courtyard.

Still, the sun blazes like a snail
across our twin foreheads.

BOB DYLAN

Bob Dylan,
unique,
so American,
so adrift.

Almost like Whitman loafing
today in Central Park.

Or Emily juggling metaphors
like torches on the Tonight Show.

The greatest balladeer of his generation
sent Joey, *It always seemed he got caught between
the mob and the man in blue,*
into the streets of Little Italy.

Weaving the lives of Hattie Carroll and Hurricane Carter
into a tapestry of intrigue.

Giving us hope and leopard-skin pillbox hats
just when we needed them the most.

So, how about this balladeer of ours,
like smoke breezing past saffron mirrors,
muscling squeaky saloon doors,
fashionably late for his showdown with God?

FALLING FROM GRACE

The ironic handkerchief,
Desdemona's or Othello's?

Who's irony is it, anyway?

That handkerchief on marionette strings
like some wobbly Saturday morning marionette
with googly eyes and freckles,
possibly of Irish descent?

That handkerchief
was the axis
on which his play revolved.

They didn't have Renaissance festivals
in Shakespeare's day.

So, he entertained himself with handkerchiefs
scented by impossible love
falling from grace.

DESTINY

Each poem has its feral destiny.

So, why interfere?

Intellectual leaps are obtained
through blind faith, anyway.

Or, we could continue slinging
fresh feces from behind the bars
of our miserable cages.

A QUICK LOOK AT DESPAIR

Amidst all this debris
I have a life.

Such as it is or will be
at my age.

Amidst all the disappointments
that educated professionalism brings.

I fly in every direction!

My ultimate freedom
and despair.

FOR THE OLD POETS

I couldn't do anything
if it weren't for you
up there
out there
beside me —
wherever it is
you call home.

You expanded the cosmos
with a feral curiosity
while writing the greatest poems
imaginable.

You invented raucous irony and the most
god-awful misery known to humankind.

You did what kings only dreamed of doing.

You explored what imagination,
the true king,
required.

It's because of you
that we challenge Lucifer, today,
with all his pet cobras,
and Jesse James
pumping bigotry from a Confederate revolver.

You built a bridge,
Walt Whitman's,
Father of American poetry,
across a dangerous river
called Democracy and Imperialism.

You cruised Walt's lonely piers
looking for signs of life.

Walt beholding the 20th century,
years before his time.

There are others, Beddoes, Bécquer, Baudelaire
and Blake — to name a few B's — those
luminous lunatics allowed to roam diasporas
while youthful armies plundered ancient cities.

Truth of the matter is, poets enjoy the slightest vibration
transmitted by every astral fiber in the universe.

RUMI SPEAKS

A carpet shadow
resembles a tiger moth.

Rumi says, *It could be the Holy One,*
or it could mean that your carpet
needs a good cleaning.

You decide.

MARLON BRANDO

Marlon said, *Not interested!*

That's the way it goes.

Run our country, literally, figuratively,
into the ground — see if it helps.

But I'm thinking (said Marlon)
there's another way, which explains
my characters wearing pasta strainers
for hats, plus ironic ponchos, perfumed scarves,
granny get-ups, and other sundry disguises.

Indeed, I possess a melancholy frivolity.

Why don't you?

PINOT NOIR

Redwood Creek, Pinot Noir, 2002,
drinks well beyond her price tag.

This full-bodied ruby flower
teases and hints of a Keats favorite.

Her hips, like the chestnut mare's on which
private schoolgirls circle the muddy paddock,
force the tubercular moon to cough
into a white handkerchief.

This Redwood Creek, Pinot Noir, 2002,
drinks well beyond her price tag.

Part III

It is the moon that dances
in the courtyard of the dead.

Look at his spent body,
blackened with shadows and wolves.

~Federico García Lorca
(trans. by W.S. Merwin)

Charles P. Hayes: "Grey Sky Moon"

IN LOVE WITH THE UNIVERSE

I need to back down
this ladder,
this extension ladder leaning
against a yellow grapefruit tree
sheltered by the filthy green hair
of Spanish moss dripping
from Tampa pines.

Why I need to back down
remains a mystery.

But I'll back down just the same
if you promise
to uphold your end
of the bargain.

No more vengeful wars,
and no more former hostages
sporting purple hearts
while escorting grieving First Ladies
who to this day mistrust the wild
but steady hands
of delinquent poets
still in love with the universe.

ODE TO OUR LEGAL SYSTEM

Theoretically, I could sink my teeth into
this velveteen cream, rust and cocoa sofa.

Yeah, well, don't ask,
don't tell.

Jesus, what kind of law
is that?

Pretend not to notice
and the gay cloud will pass?

As for my teeth,
they're a million miles away.

ARIEL

Ariel was a pirate ship.

Think.

Shelley and Byron hatching a new world order?

The Crown was more than a little cranky.

The King might've been onto Blake, too,
but wagered his illusion
on William's early infatuation
with Swedenborg angels and vengeful gods.

But, *Ariel* sliced through moonlit clouds
of revolution as easily
as any young mother giving birth to hope
and humanity.

Not so popular, this new world order,
with the British Crown.

Then *Ariel* set out one day
on the Gulf of Spezia,
one calm blue day.

TWIST OF FATE

Did you feel that quake, that transition
into a new age?

A minor speed bump,
as reminder?

Me, either.

So, what's all this hype about clocks
measuring years according to the earth's rotation?

Is this the best way
to calibrate our lives?

Perhaps.

Here comes that taxi, that checkered caterpillar,
skittering across winter cobblestones, Louisville,
early 1950s.

Driver, hair coiled into a hornet's nest,
identification card
faded beyond recognition.

The cab pants over frozen rice paddies
glistening beneath amber streetlights.

Finally, we enter the green intersection
like convicts adored by the Walt Disney Corporation,
or 17-year cicadas drilling holes
into religious wallpaper for woodpeckers.

We emerge intact.

Still, who's that mucking with our precious
oil reserves?

Those sad life and death reserves spoon-fed like cod liver oil
by judges' black wings folded tightly against the *Bible*?

So many yachts weave the Milky Way.

Too many to count,
like bobbing senators on Long Island Sound after midnight.

DNA

*

Gregor ends up alone in his room
while his family flees the apartment.

You can draw a parallel from Gregor
to the Hunger Artist vaporized
into a stain on a bed of straw.

A stain on a bed of straw.

*****

You flash scarab eyes
while yelling at the moon.

The primary supporters of the Catholic Church
are out tonight,
hunting 12-point bucks.

However, a shabby antler,
one fractured along its tip by stray bullet,
won't suffice.

For these professional odds-makers,
or gods-makers,
demand mythical perfection,
and they won't settle for less.

Can you blame them?

Blame them for what?

Blame them for achieving the primary goal
of wealth at any cost,

tumbling like nuclear dice across the velvet waists
of Las Vegas craps tables?

So, why demean the wild fly
feasting on a dog turd?

Explain that one,
and I'll answer those nagging questions
about the universe.

Even the bonus question,
the one about humans spooning monkey brains
from the diminutive skulls of political machismo.

24.

Made it to 24!

Hailed a taxi for the last 12 miles of the Boston Marathon
and saw my career spinning in a dryer
near Grolier's bookstore
stocked to the ceiling
with angels'
bright fins
igniting the dark shadows
of forbidden shelves.

44.

The end of an era.

The best of the best
gone to their graves
wondering, wondering
if they ever were
worthy of such mythical praise
in the first place.

133.

Imagine wondering about that?

Imagine wondering about the speed
of the psyche?

Is the psyche more the jade spark
of a lusty firefly
or the enchanted psychology of a leopard slug grazing cabbage
    leaves?

Is it the irrational
spray of machine guns
in our schoolyards,
in our movie theaters,
in our traditional solution
for all the problems of the world?

ξ ψ ж

Or is it, merely,
the unavoidable amnesia inherited
from our one true god,
DNA?

GOOD FORTUNE

(I…I'll put a gun in your face.
You'll pay with your life!)
              --Jagger and Richards

Speaking of good fortune,
did you hear the one
about the Czechoslovakian priest and a camel?

Me, either.

Meanwhile, hours, like white mice on a bar of soap,
gnaw the final bits of darkness from the dawn.

Good fortune?

I…I got a debt to repay.
I ain't gonna lie!

Sometimes good fortune
plays by its own rules;
but, then, how is that good fortune?

Oops! Didn't mean to get political.

I guess good fortune's
whatever your high-priced militia can afford.

ODE TO A MOVIE DIRECTOR

He's either the lover
or the killer —
all depends whose side
you're on.

Ask him for intellectual ID
and he'll flash a brilliant disguise.

Ask him for emotional DNA
and he'll vanish like a cougar
into the receding hairline
of Hollywood, California.

ODE TO JACKIE ROBINSON

Papa Joe's *Big Red*
is my kinda merlot.

Like koi tippling the muscular surface
of a Columbian cartel's serpentine pond
shadowed by Roman statues cupping
algae-covered breasts and pissing on the hyacinths.

This merlot,
sister or lover?

You decide.

Fate was never
my strong suit.

This fate who never ceases to amaze.

This fate who once threw spitballs at God's
heavily-padded shinbones blocking the plate
whenever Jackie Robinson
tried to steal home.

This fate beside me this very moment,
tipping her third crystal glass
of Papa Joe's *Big Red*.

A VERY BAD POEM

(For Alan Britt)

That poem had its war bonnet on.

Its bald eagle feathers bloodstained,
with some quasi Duende
hissing at mythology.

It even waved its spear like Blake
shaking his fist at the wretched stars!

Yes, sir. That poem
had all the right intentions.

POET TO HIS DOG

Let me tell you something—
it's hard to come up
with clever stuff 100 times a day!

Your buffet meals alone
keep me hopping.

Not to mention all those car rides
to supermarket, post office
and private school
for number one daughter.

You love to hang out.

I'm amazed you prefer a bumpy backseat,
sloshing puddles and oozing muddy stops,
to dozing in the bedroom,
living room, the cinnamon hallway,
or upon our cool lemon bathroom tiles.

Given that our DNA's are so darn close,
it's a wonder I don't enjoy
gnawing my own hind leg
or circling the yard with a white plastic,
five-gallon bucket in my mouth.

Ah, your impetuous nature
is forever my gain, my friend.

Here, let me loosen your tie-dyed collar.

Your love is forever my gain,
my dearest friend.

SHRED OF EVIDENCE

I'm prepared to die singing.

You might think
I'm better off saving my breath
for the crapshoot of the millennium
that'll never happen.

But, understand,
lobbyists huff loaded dice
down long, checkered corridors
before slinging them across the halls of Congress,
or History, as it's come to be known.

Somewhere in the Yellowstone Mountains
lives a wolf,
a mythical,
humble wolf,
part Republican,
part Socialist,
but a wolf,
nonetheless.

This wolf gnaws the leg bone
of hope,
our final shred
of evidence.

EVOLUTION

Nuances are what we value most—
concepts littered with opaque symbols.

Nuances.

Obscure philosophies and their erudite philosophers twitching
like nervous zebras at the shrinking waterhole of existence,
until tired saxophones, those thirsty elephants of hope,
stumble upon the vanishing waterhole
of unrequited love.

Perhaps the most misunderstood of them all.

Unrequited love.

How can we ever forget it?

If Darwin is correct,
we never will.

THE CORNER OF EDMONDSON AND NORTHERN PARKWAY

As the small-town circus clown said to the oil executive,
I'm joyously fucked up! But, you, how do you sleep inside
your acorn skull frozen by February blasts? How do you live?

Fortunately, I don't require bullshit rhetoric to navigate
like a cinnamon panther the palmettos and mythical stars
of my ancient Seminole village.

Instead, I rely on baby alligators to rip clots from my vital
arteries; otherwise, I might as well feign amnesia, today,
on this faded, forest green MTA bench at the corner
of Edmondson and Northern Parkway.

IN-BETWEEN LIVES

I'm in-between lives,
trapped in some time-warped mirror,
just visiting
Glen Miller Park
with its thatched, peeling, emerald picnic stables,
Richmond, Indiana,
all the while
thinking
that Richmond, Indiana,
to the universe
is like Jupiter
to planet Earth.

I find I'm tempted
by tornadoes,
mostly,
but not so much
by vague hurricanes
way up here in Hoosierville.

(Though I reside inside the beating heart
of democracy, Reisterstown, Maryland.)

But I absorb history just the same,
like a sponge
torn loose from its reef
and drifting
below a coral cluster
of parrot greens and algae blues.

Some nights, feigning courage, I'm known
to shuffle beyond the porch
in moose-skin slippers resembling
flamingoes skimming their hooked beaks
backwards in twilight just
below the mirrored surface of survival.

AMERICAN POLITICS

(For Red Cloud)

You know it doesn't matter
who's President.

The President doesn't control
the death rate, anyway.

Take genocide, for example.

Not long ago, *both* parties disguised
cholera as truth, then quarantined
Sioux grandmothers and babies
inside buffalo skins stretched
across warm, moist South Dakota
nights punctuated by insane bullfrogs.

Part IV

I've been there
Where the dead
Are not buried,
But their bones
Write laws
Controlling love,
Write books of etiquette
For the polite thieves
Of life.

~Duane Locke

Charles P. Hayes: "Birdpoint"

VARIOUS DISGUISES

When you believe you've outsmarted death,
you inherit the most trouble.

Things appear out of the ordinary,
and that's just the beginning.

Phenomenology should clarify, but daily experience
proves as elusive as krill navigating
the baleen plates of a blue whale
rustling the southern coast off Sri Lanka.

Yet, existence mimics earthly possessions, too:
immaculate stereo speakers hand-built in Nashville,
Tennessee exhaling a muscular poetry more potent
than 19th century proselytizing composers
sentimentalizing their dimwitted youth
into a nationalist frenzy.

Unless you're a great blue whale from Newcastle,
Indiana, that is, heading straight for the Senior Special
at rush hour, just before the 50-millimeter Iraqi round
dissects your eldest grandson's liver into perfect fillets
of smoked salmon at a Vegas munitions tradeshow.

Ah, well, analogies don't exist any more than
sentimental halters leading us to baptism, our daily
bucket of oats, providing us with religious shelter,
and all at the expense of the rancid truth
camouflaged in black and blue whale disguises.

BEETHOVEN'S EARDRUMS

(Andante con moto quasi Allegretto)
--by LVB

With a fawn Bouvier,
unironed laundry
expels oxygen
that irritates the strings
of Beethoven violins,
with Ludwig's ear canals
virtually clogged
by the French Revolution
and fate sealed
tighter than Baudelaire's
weekly visits
to Parisian whores—
unconcerned
with the Count's empty threats,
Ludwig rebuffed the Count's
overtures again and again.

SHIT HAPPENS WHEN YOU'RE A DOG

Shit happens when you're a dog.

You have only 10 to 12 years
of intensity.

If you're lucky,
your final years
involve compassionate survival.

Compassion, ah, there's the rub.

Has to be a rub somewhere;
otherwise, dreadful expectations
could relieve themselves
like drunken patrons
stumbling from taverns
on the outskirts,
heading home
for more wine.

Dogs are subject to potluck
in such situations.

Although dogs pretty much
wake up whenever they please,
and when they do,
it's, *Are you hungry?*
or, *You wanna go outside?*

But dogs also gather the logs
necessary for our winter fireplaces.

Blue flames pop
from their loving fur.

FRIDAY NIGHT, LATE SEPTEMBER

I weave like a boa
through laundry hanging
on pastel plastic hangers
from basement coppers,
quarter-inch leads
Eschering my jungle of existence.

I could collapse
beneath these humid, black cotton trousers
and heavy, grey sweats,
even choke on these button-downs
that never realized expectations.

But I choose
to stand, anyway.

I cut through
all the bullshit
to live another day.

JIMI HENDRIX

His legacy, six tortured
guitar strings.

Rattlesnakes of sensibility
curling arthritic fingers into bony fists
of Supreme Court Justices
out for a good Halloween joke.

Jimi's irony lingers
like a Peruvian jaguar
partially hidden below thick palmettos,
like Rousseau's Noble Savage
expecting to receive everything
except the solemn
blessing of the Lord,
since the Lord's blessing
is not yet reserved for wild animals.

And so remains
a certain lack of sophistication in our culture,
except for blessed Shiraz's
ruby rain
scrubbing the cobblestones
of Little Italy, Baltimore,
September 24,
another sacred day of our Lord.

Anyway, Jimi was all amperage;
volts didn't matter.

Jimi was completely free to tackle governments
and reconstruct
the youth culture.

Which is what made him
dangerous in the first place.

GERONIMO'S RAID

It's almost like a dawn raid
by Geronimo against a Mexican village
peacefully asleep,
so far as anyone knew,
so far as the babies knew.

Even today, surprise raids
disturb the Pentagon enjoying
otherwise hospitable affairs
with nefarious dictators,
so far as anyone knows.

I'm almost of a mind to declare Marshall Law
against Geronimo, except for legends
about his brujo soul creeping
like genocidal smoke
across the beautiful crags and crevices
of our 19th century immigrant foreheads.

It's almost like a dawn raid
by Geronimo against a Mexican village,
babies sleeping, so far as they knew,
so far as anyone knew.

PARTISAN OBJECTIONS

I remember years of grief
before the joy began.

Long before the moon dug its rhinoceros horn
between dawn's diaphanous thighs
spread-eagle across my rooftop.

I remember days
we'd all like to forget.

Candy cane bellbottoms
outlining Long Island fog
don't begin to tell the story.

Too many aperitifs, I suppose,
at favorite Italian restaurants.

There's a discovery on Quasar Five—
time to resign my life (such as it is) to a black
tuft of Bouvier fur abandoned like a diminutive
storm cloud across our sacred basement's
Burberry carpet.

But, by god, each time we travel below these acid
clouds fueled by gravity's lithium kisses,
we pass desperately close
to my partisan objections.

ULTIMATE INNOCENCE

Last farmer wholly in love
with his milk cows?

1860s, you think?

1914, thereabouts?

Or could've been the dustbowl years
before FDR's sympathetic intervention.

Too bad Gene Wilder's taxi
circling the moon
tossed him onto cold skid row
to slake his lust
with a trembling drop
of Woolite.

Sorry about that!

Too bad a Confederate train
snaking the Blue Ridge
didn't pause
long enough for its boxcars of genetic mules
to slake
themselves on tourist ticket stubs.

So, how do we climb
like Buddhist gardenias
the sultry torso of present-day civilization
during a natural disaster
named Katrina or George W. Bush?

How, indeed, to skate the length
of this melancholy ironing board

stretched yoga-like before us?

And how to know
when white polo balls
flattened into retirement
won't grow extinct like dirty mushrooms
ignored by our distracted selves along the produce aisle?

Who knows?

So, I mounted that black and white pinto
I'd been dreaming about
these past six months.

He said, *Let's go to the canyons*
of the outlaws:
Wyoming, Utah,
Tombstone, Colorado or Kerouac;
I'd like that.

But, instead, I reached for Saturn,
ignored these past 50 years,
only to find her metallic rings squashed
into an ashtray,
only to witness
the demise
of briefly
what once was
the innocence
of furious crows
oozing tiny drops
of insidious ink
from my adult imagination.

THE MOLAR

*

Sweep away that feeble molar,
that decayed root canal.

Get the broom
and sweep for all you're worth!

Muck the stalls;
it's Friday!

Sweep away indecisions
debilitating your life.

Sweep away those nasty political centipedes
breeding complacency.

Sweep away the savoy truffle
of indiscretionary years.

**

Water damage always puts me
on alert.

***

When the volcano erupted,
I remember now,
we were huddled below a fresco,
a tattoo
of mythical proportion
every bit as symbolic
as our universe
appears to be

today.

****

So, sweep away that feeble molar
lazing in a hammock
near a root canal.

Get the broom
and sweep for all you're worth!

THE APPALOOSA

Ride that appaloosa
through the Black Forest
of primordial fears.

Glide her granite hips
past neon cocktail glasses
rocking seaside taverns
you'd like to forget
now that 50 years
of Atlantic undertow
has you
behaving
like a
marionette
on acid.

Ride
because
you must;
feel the sway
of appaloosa
beneath you!

EVERYONE WANTS TO BURN

Every day I devote myself
to her,
thunder shreds
my gauze dining room curtains;
bison clouds
nudge power lines past suburban warehouses.

Everyone wants to burn
as bright as blue plumes
billowing I-95 Philadelphia
sanitation incinerators,
7 AM,
rush hour.

But, today, the road not taken
is the only road left.

So, fellow horses of instruction,
shake your gilded halters,
but beware
that beautiful blue wolves prowl these beautiful blue hills
we're so fond of calling home,
and remember that the scam often unfolds
when you least expect it.

However, for the scam to become a sanctified scam
it must first pass the test of guard dogs
fast asleep on Sunday piles of unironed laundry.

But, let me tell you,
78 pounds of herding dog can relax
like no one's business atop wrinkled denim asses
and ungodly wads of barracuda-striped business shirts
quietly shielding at least three pairs
of slightly-stained and exhausted khaki illusions.

AFTER THE CIVIL WAR

Reconstruction,
as I recall.

Reconstruction
that followed families
throughout Louisiana bayous
of the Coushatta nation.

Reconstruction
that involved your folks
and mine.

Yet, not a single great aunt
voted for the tattered flag
that day,
let alone
baked a pie,
a special,
nonpartisan pie
that everyone could enjoy.

GETTING HARD TO TELL

It's an eleven-hundred-dollar bottle
of Chilean merlot, or perhaps
Papa Joe's *Big Red*
signaling
from a buoy disguised
as a mermaid below the moonlit Atlantic.

I used to worship
the clouded berries
of your seaweed hair
before godmother invaded
my Brothers Grimm romance,
prowling my sheets and pillowcases.

I used to worship
uncanny freedom
until I stumbled
across guilt and despair,
not necessarily in that order.

Dressed as a male peacock,
shimmering for all he's worth,
I worshiped electric imagination.

And, sometimes, I even worshipped the Divine Providence
promised by a bloody placenta
sprawled like autumn across the granary floor
of a 19th century metaphor.

I worshipped it all!

Then rode like hell, one god-awful night,
my ghostly appaloosa and I,
across the feral penumbra,
bleeding from our genocidal blue eyes.

LATE SEPTEMBER AUBADE

Relaxing at 2:09 AM is kinda like
wading right through,
without a sacred toga,
right through the tribunal.

Naked.

Into the court
of injustice
with puffy councilmen.

All throughout the 16th century,
those puffy councilmen
dreamed of 15th-century whores
draped in oily linens
licked clean by flinty lanterns.

Which reminds me,
who makes the best avocado
sandwich brimming
alfalfa sprouts'
copperheads
and boomslange new age garters
resembling the moment
of conception,
wriggling,
hurling themselves
against the rocks
like harbor seals
gone mad
or driven just plain crazy
by the San Francisco
legislature?

FOR GEORGE

George eases his slide
into Gary Moore's
"That Kind of Woman."

Sneaks in, sans wah wah,
three quick licks,
then leans back into
a Bonnie Raitt sultry riff.

Brass on steel suggests
"Apple Scruffs" or "Layla"
as his Gretsch grinds its
antlers against the elephant
trunk of a thorny acacia.

He's no yearling,
this George Harrison,
though hairless now
and staggering
through the gilded halls
of the Almighty.

A blue note from George's guitar
sparks the nearby stall
of a nearby barn
igniting nearby hay.

Soon the entire barn is ablaze.

Raul Villallreal (Cover painting: *No Longer (IN)Visible, acrylic and oil on canvas, 48" x 36"*)

Raúl Villarreal was born in San Francisco de Paula, Havana, Cuba in 1964. He emigrated with his family to Madrid, Spain in 1972; two years later, the family moved to the United States, settling in Union City, New Jersey. Over the past 25 years Villarreal has exhibited his art in 20 one person exhibits and over 400 group exhibits in the United States, Canada, Cuba, Costa Rica, Germany, Italy, Spain and China. Villarreal's book, *Hemingway's Cuban Son*, based on his father René's memoirs of his friendship with the famous American author was published by **The Kent State University Press** in March of 2009. For the last five years Villarreal has presented the book throughout the United States, the **Hemingway Museum** in Havana, Cuba, plus **International Hemingway Conferences** in Ronda, Spain and Lausanne, Switzerland.

Villarreal received his M.F.A. in 2005 from New Jersey City University, Jersey City, New Jersey. He has taught at Mason Gross School of the Arts at Rutgers University, Seton Hall University, New Jersey City University, College of Saint Elizabeth and the County College of Morris. He serves on the Advisory Board at the **Center for Latino Arts and Culture** at Rutgers University in New Brunswick and for the **Therese A. Maloney Art Gallery** at the College of Saint Elizabeth in Morristown, New Jersey.

Villarreal's oeuvre is inspired by personal memories and experiences of growing up in Cuba, Spain and the United States, along with the assimilation of other cultures, appropriated images from mass media, and old family photographs. Utilizing personal iconography, through assemblages and a process of layering of these different elements, Villarreal attempts to convey a sense of multiple realities, time references, and existence. The works address issues of identity, multiculturalism and transculturalism.

Raúl Villarreal: www.raulvillarreal

Charles P. Hayes (Photographs)

Charles Hayes is a writer and photographer who received his MA from the University of New Mexico in Art Therapy in 1989. In 1978, his book, *From the Hudson to the World, Voices of the River* was introduced by Pete Seeger and published by Seeger's **Hudson River Clearwater Sloop Restoration**. Hayes also helped edit and did translations for the book *For Neruda, For Chile* edited by Walter Lowenfels and published by **Beacon Press**. Hayes' essays and poetry have been published in various magazines including *Ann Arbor Review, Bicycle Review, Poetry Review, The Smith* and *University of Tampa Review*. His ongoing interviews with artists and writers, which began in the 80s, were recently published in *Ragazine* (www.ragazine.cc) starting with his interviews with John Cage (1984) and Dorothy Rockburne (2014).

Hayes' photographs have been exhibited in various galleries in New Jersey and New York, including most recently at **Gallery on the Green**, Madison, NJ, **WPA Gallery** at Pound Ridge Reservation, Pound Ridge, NY, the **Bean Runner Gallery Café**, Peekskill, NY and **Barnes & Nobel Booksellers**, Cortlandt, NY. He photographed the cover for the 2007 international music CD, *Beyond Borders*, published by *International Gallerie* of Mumbai, India. He's worked as photographer for the **City of Peekskill on the Hudson**, and has extensively photographed performances by violinist and composer, Daisy Jopling. Hayes authored the photo-driven essay, "Shopping for Booties in Newtown" on the slayings at Sandy Hook, CT. His photo-essay is available at http://www.thebicyclereview.net/stories-archive-vol-ii.html.

Presently, he is editing the sequel to *From the Hudson to the World, Voices of the River* in a 21st century anthology entitled, *Voices of the River: To Pete Seeger*.

Alan Britt (Poetry)

Alan Britt served as judge for the **2013 The Bitter Oleander Press Library of Poetry Book Award**. He read poetry and presented "Modern Trends in U.S. Poetry" at the **VII International Writers' Festival** in Val-David, Canada, May 2013. His interview at **The Library of Congress** for *The Poet and the Poem* aired on **Pacifica Radio,** January 2013. Recent interviews appeared in *Lake City Lights, Minnesota Review, Published-to-be: The Forum of Aspiring Writers* and *Steaua Cultural Review* (Romania). He read poems at the **Fountain Street Fine Art Gallery** in Framingham, MA (2014); for *Oasis: An Evening of Music & Poetry* presented by **La Ruche Arts Contemporary Consortium** at the **Union City Museum of Art/William V. Musto Cultural Center**, Union City, NJ (2014); at the historic **Maysles Cinema** in Harlem/NYC (2013), and at the **World Trade Center/Tribute WTC Visitor Center** in Manhattan/NYC (2012).

Britt has published 14 books of poetry: *Lost Among the Hours* (2015), *Parabola Dreams* (with Silvia Scheibli: 2013), *Alone with the Terrible Universe* (2011), *Greatest Hits* (2010), *Hurricane* (2010), *Vegetable Love* (2009), *Vermilion* (2006), *Infinite Days* (2003), *Amnesia Tango* (1998), *Bodies of Lightning* (1995), *The Afternoon of the Light* (1981), *I Suppose the Darkness Is Ours* (1977), *Ashes in the Flesh* (1976) and *I Ask for Silence Also* (1969). His poem "One Life to Live" was selected by *Crack the Spine Literary Magazine* for *Best of the Net Anthology 2014* for Sundress Publications. His poems "Drinking Red Wine and Thinking About Nomenclature" and "Driving Through Bartow, Florida" won **The Big Rock Candy Award** and **The Florida Poetry Contest** sponsored by the *Hobo Camp Review* and *The Florida Review* respectively. He is Poetry Editor for the **We Are You Project International** (www.weareyouproject.org) and Book Review Editor for *Ragazine* (www.ragazine.cc).

Selected readings include **Folger Shakespeare Library** (Washington, DC), **WEDU** (PBS Television), **ABC Radio National** (Australian Broadcasting Corporation), **PCA/ACA Conference** (Boston),

88

Wilmer Jennings Gallery (East Village/NYC), **University at Albany/SUNY, WPA Gallery at Pound Ridge Reservation**, (Pound Ridge, NY), **NCTE: Afro-American Read-In** (Towson University), **The Goethe Institute** (Washington, DC), **The Writer's Center** (Bethesda, MD), **MICA** (Maryland Institute College of Art), **New Jersey City University**, and **Ramapo College**. He received his Master's Degree from The Johns Hopkins University Writing Seminars and currently teaches English/Creative Writing at Towson University.

Links: The Wiki Literary Underground: http://theliteraryunderground.org/wiki/index.php?title=Alan_Britt

Alan Britt: http://alanbritt.wordpress.com/

Daphne (See page 36)

Photograph by MaryBeth Britt

Daphne is a fawn Bouvier des Flandres. She is currently 11 years old. She fancies the above photo which captures her with a fresh summer haircut as a gorgeous, strapping 4-year-old. She's a sensitive, loving and highly intelligent soul who takes pride in patrolling the perimeters of her property making sure that uninvited guests such as prowlers, squirrels and sneaky groundhogs do not violate the confines of her territory. She's not overly fond of rabbits, but she can't catch them, so . . . . She does bark at the occasional school bus, dump truck and UPS van for good measure. She herds them, in fact. It's in her DNA since they, too, must understand exactly who's in charge. During walks around the neighborhood she often attracts attention, causing people stop and point in awe of her impressive beauty. In short, she's the best!

CREDITS:

Rain Mountain Press

Fiction, Poetry, Nonfiction

Fiction (Selected)

Shriver by Chris Belden: (ISBN: 978-0-9853-0125-5)
Insect Dreams by Rosalind Palermo Stevenson:
                                              (ISBN: 978-0-9786-1052-4)
Eilat by Luna Tarlo: (ISBN: 978-0-9786-1056-2)
The Taste of Fog by David Chorlton: (ISBN: 978-0-9834-7832-4)
Third Wife by Jiri Klobouk: (ISBN: 978-0-9853-0120-0)
Port Authority Orchids by Stephanie Dickinson:
                                              (ISBN: 978-0-9853-0129-3)
Mostly Beethoven by Jiri Klobouk, short Story, Pocket Series:
                                              (ISBN: 978-1-4951-0603-3)
Kafka at Rudolf Steiner's by Rosalind Palermo Stevenson, short
story: (ISBN: 978-0-9897-0519-6)

Poetry (Selected)

Cities Hidden by Rain by Edgar Cage: (ISBN: 978-0-9897-0513-4)
*Graduating from Eternity by John Goode:
                                         (ISBN: 978-0-9853-0128-6)
Mosquito Operas by Philip Dacey: (ISBN: 978-0-9802-2116-9)
Church of the Adagio by Philip Dacey: (ISBN: 978-0-9897-0514-1)
*No Brainer Variations by Jim Cory: (ISBN: 978-0-9802-2118-3)
Blitzkrieg by John Gosslee: (ISBN: 978-0-9897-0511-0)
A Blanquito In El Barrio by Gil Fagiani: (ISBN: 978-0-9802-2113-8)
Songs for the Extinction of Winter by Rob Cook:
                                         (ISBN: 978-0-9786-1059-3)

Escape to Nowhere by Flower Conroy: (ISBN: 978-0-9834-7831-7)
So Late into the Night by Elinor Nauen: (ISBN: 978-0-9802-2114-5)
Under Taos Mountain by Penelope Scambly Schott:
                                       (ISBN: 978-0-9802-2115-2)
The Short Imposition of Living by Matthew Keuter:
                                       (ISBN: 978-0-9802-2110-7)
The Complete Cinnamon Bay Sonnets by Andrew Kaufman:
                                       (ISBN: 978-0-9897-0515-8)
Long Way Back to the End by Paul B. Roth:
                                       (ISBN: 978-0-9897-0516-5)
asking my liver for forgiveness by Rob Cook:
                                       (ISBN: 978-0-9897-0517-2)
Lightning's Dance Floor by Ronald Wardall:
                                       (ISBN: 978-0-9802 2119-0)
Lost Among the Hours by Alan Britt: (ISBN: 978-1-4951-0606-4)
Force of Flesh by Linda Tieber: (ISBN: 978-1-4951-0604-0)

*The Ronald Wardall Series

Nonfiction

The King of White Collar Boxing (A Memoir) by David Lawrece:
                                       (ISBN: 978-0-9834-7833-1)
My Father's Window by Maya Mary Hebert:

                                       (ISBN: 978-0-9786-1054-8)

Rain Mountain Press

68 East Third Street, Suite 16
New York, NY 10003
USA
www.rainmountainpress.com
info@rainmountainpress.com